U.S. Navy Ships Camouflage W
Destroyers and Destroyer Esco

by Al Adcock

Squadron Signal® Publications

Covers and art by Don Greer

Credits

- U.S. Navy
- Real War Photos
- U.S. National Archives
- The Floating Drydock
- ELSILRAC
- U.S. Coast Guard

All photos used in this publication are official U.S. Navy photos that have been declassified and provided by various individuals and official U.S. government sources.

ISBN 978-0-89747-571-6

Military/Combat Photographs

If you have any photos of aircraft, armor, soldiers, or ships of any nation, particularly wartime snapshots, why not share them with us and help make Squadron/Signal's books all the more interesting and complete in the future? Any photograph sent to us will be copied and returned. Electronic images are preferred. The donor will be fully credited for any photos used. Please send them to:

Squadron/Signal Publications
1115 Crowley Drive, Carrollton, TX 75006-1312 U.S.A.
www.SquadronSignalPublications.com

--

About the Special Series

Squadron/Signal Publications' most open-ended genre of books, our Special category features a myriad of subjects that include unit histories, military campaigns, aircraft, ships, armor, and uniforms. Upcoming subjects include war heroes and non-military areas of interest. If you have an idea for a book or are interested in authoring one, please let us know.

(Front Cover) The GAINARD (DD-706) an ALLEN M. SUMNER Class destroyer, was camouflaged in Measure 31/16d, the Dark Pattern System, as applied in 1944. The colors used were Haze Gray (5-H), Ocean Gray (5-O), and Dull Black (BK), on the vertical surfaces, with the deck painted in patterns of Ocean gray and Deck Blue (20-B).

(Title Page) The FOOTE (DD-511), camouflaged in Measure 32/18d, the Medium Pattern System, sails past the Los Angeles Harbor Light, San Pedro Breakwater, known as Angel's Gate, in 1944. The FOOTE was a FLETCHER Class (DD-448) five-gun destroyer that operated first in the Atlantic and later in the Pacific Area of Operation, earning four Battle Stars. A pair of net tenders prepare to close the net designed to stop enemy submarines from entering the harbor. (Floating Dry Dock)

(Back Cover) The USS BOYD (DD-544), in the foreground, and the USS CRAVEN (DD-382), in the background cruise through the Pacific Ocean on their way to the Wake Island Raid. DD-544 received 11 Battle Stars for its WWII service and five Battle Stars for its service in Korea. The DD-382 received nine Battle Stars for its WWII service.

INTRODUCTION

Since the formation of the Continental Navy in 1775, U.S. Navy ships have worn a variety of colors, from black to white. The purpose of the colors was originally either to seal the wood or to have a cooling effect for the interior of the ships. Early U.S. destroyers were painted in black or dark gray and experiments were actually undertaken in the Philippines in 1915 in which the BAINBRIDGE (DD-1) was painted in panels of light and dark grays.

The art of camouflage did not come into play until World War I (WWI, 1914-1918) when the German submarine menace, in the form of the U-Boat, threatened to stop the flow of supplies being sent by the United States and Canada to support the Allied war effort in Europe. The Royal Navy began using a splinter type camouflage to confuse the enemy as to speed, distance, and course on their ships.

The U.S. Navy also began to employ camouflage schemes similar to those of the Royal Navy during WWI. The Bureau of Construction and Repair (C & R) produced 193 designs for U.S. Navy ships, mostly for destroyers. These early designs were the work of Everett Warner, who would also produce designs employed during World War II (WWII, 1939-1945). Blues, grays, black, purple, and even yellow were used in the schemes. The idea of camouflaging warships spilled over into the civilian shipping community when cargo and ship insurance added an additional wartime premium to vessels that were not camouflaged. The civilian ships were camouflaged in the warship colors, but with yellows and reds added to the blues, grays, and black schemes. An array of colorful ships thus adorned the wartime seas.

During 1918, most U.S. destroyers operating in the Atlantic wore some type of "splinter" or, as it was called, "piebald," schemes. After the end of hostilities in Europe, the U.S. Navy painted over the camouflage schemes with dark or light grays at the discretion of the area commanders. In 1928 a color called #5 Standard Navy Gray was adopted and was used until 1940 on most ships.

The U.S. Navy became serious about camouflage when the Bureau of Construction and Repairs issued instructions in its publication *C&R-4* in 1937. The *C&R-4* provided for dazzle paint, false bow waves, false ship perspective, and painting stacks black or white. January

Destroyer Number 1, the BAINBRIDGE, sails off of Olongpo, the Philippines in 1915. She is camouflaged with what appear to be panels of dark gray, light gray, and dark blue. It is believed that this is one of the first examples of an attempt to camouflage a U.S. Navy destroyer. Very early U.S. destroyers were basically torpedo boats, as their main function was to scout and protect the fleet. (Elsilrac)

1941 saw the introduction of *Ships-2,* which defined the colors and application of Measures 1 through 9, with the terms Measures and Systems used interchangeably. Measures 1 through 5 concerned destroyers, while the rest (6 through 9) addressed cruisers and submarines. The term Measure could be abbreviated as MS and Measure and scheme could be interchanged.

Subsequent instructions issued in September 1941, June 1942, March 1943, June 1943, and March 1945 added more new designs that eventually would number 33 individual camouflage paint Measures and schemes.

During 1940 and 1941, before the start of the war in the Pacific, the U.S. Navy undertook experiments in the Territory of Hawaii. Various color schemes were painted on destroyers of Destroyer Squadron Five (DesRon 5) to test the effectiveness of Sea Blue (5-S), Navy Blue (5-N), Sapphire Blue (Measure 1-B), and alternate colors for Measure 2. Following the tests, it was reported that Sea Blue (5-S) painted on all vertical surfaces, and Deck Blue (20-D) on all horizontal surfaces offered the best protection from air or sea observers. Sapphire Blue was also considered desirable, but the paint faded too quickly.

There were also many unofficial schemes. Cavite Blue was painted on U.S. ships that were making their way south from the Philippines to Australia in early 1942. The year 1942 also saw the introduction of Mountbatten Pink, a Lavender-Gray scheme, sometimes called Plymouth Pink, that had been adopted by Lord Louis Mountbatten and applied on his British Destroyer Squadron vessels. During a transit from the Pacific to the Atlantic, the WINSLOW (DD-359) stopped in Cape Town, South Africa, for resupply. While in port, her worn Sapphire Blue scheme was painted over in Mountbatten Pink, a color derived from the Union-Castle Shipping Lines' lavender paint.

During WWII, U.S. Navy destroyers wore many camouflage schemes, from blue to gray, black to painted bow wave, and multiple dazzle schemes. When the war ended in 1945, the Navy went back to the Standard Navy Gray, now known as Measure 27, formerly Measure 13 (5-H Haze Gray) for all destroyers, thus concluding the era of camouflage, although some destroyers were still spotted in Measure 21, the Navy Blue System, and Measure 22, the Graded System, as late as 1949.

The RINGOLD, Destroyer Number 89, wears yet another "piebald" scheme that was produced for U.S. destroyers during WWI. The early schemes were produced by the Bureau of Construction and Repair and the colors were probably black or dark navy blue, that carried over the boot topping, and medium gray over the basic hull color of light gray. The RINGOLD was loaned to Great Britain in 1940 and renamed the HMS NEWARK. (Real War Photos)

The ALYWIN, Destroyer Number 47, is operating at 29.78 knots in the Atlantic Ocean during builder's trials out of Cramp Shipyard, Philadelphia, Pennsylvania, on 19 November 1914. The hull and superstructure appear to be painted a dark gray, sometimes called "battleship gray." The guns have yet to be installed, but the number 2 and number 3 gun mounts have been covered with canvas sheeting, a standard practice on these early destroyers. (Real War Photos)

The PERKINS, Destroyer Number 26, rides at anchor during WWI in 1918. She is camouflaged in one of the "piebald" schemes that were designed for U.S. destroyers during the Great War. The colors were probably dark blue and dark gray panels over the basic hull color of light gray. The tall masts were required to provide support for the short wave wire antennas. (Real War Photos)

The DENT, Destroyer Number 116, wears a scheme that painted one stack and torpedo tubes black in an attempt disguise the destroyer's class during WWI. The hull has panels of black and probably medium gray over a light gray hull. The hull number appears just below the bridge area on the main deck's weather protector. The DENT was converted to a High Speed Transport during WWII and given the new hull number APD-9. (Real War Photos)

The CALDWELL, Destroyer Number 69, operates off of Mare Island, California, on 14 December 1917. She appears to be camouflaged in the Mackay Low Visibility scheme, which was one of the many designs utilized during World War One. The brush stroke colors appear to be a medium gray over the basic hull color of light gray. (Real War Photos)

The WARD, Destroyer Number 139, from the WICKES Class wore a dazzle scheme during WWI service. The WARD was responsible for sinking a Japanese midget submarine on the morning of 7 December 1941, before the attack at Pearl Harbor, Territory of Hawaii. The WARD was converted to a High Speed Transport and was sunk on 7 December 1944 off the Philippines. (Bureau of Construction & Repairs via Floating Dry Dock)

The FOOTE (DD-511) was camouflaged in 32v11/18d, the Medium Pattern System, as drawn for the FLETCHER Class. The three colors used were the standard for the Medium Pattern design. The FOOTE was awarded four Battle Stars for her service in the Pacific.

Measure 1, The Dark Gray System

Measure 1, defined as the Dark Gray System, was authorized in the January 1941 publication of *Ships-2*, a revision of *C&R-4*. The instructions called for all vertical surfaces to be painted Dark Gray (5-D), all horizontal surfaces, except wood decks, to be painted a dark gray (5-D). All surfaces above the stacks, including masts and gun directors, were to be painted a light gray (5-L). All hull numbers were to be painted white, without shading; were to be 24 inches (60.96 mm) high; and be placed bow and stern on 2,100-ton destroyers. Hull numbers were to be 24 inches on the bow, and 15 inches (38.1mm) or 25 inches (63.5 mm) on the stern of 1,200-ton destroyers. The hull number directive also covered Measures 2 through 5 on destroyers.

The Dark Gray paint scheme was found to be very desirable because of the low reflectance of the paint used in the system, and because it offered low visibility to surface and aerial observers. Nonetheless, when the September 1941 *Ships-2* publication was issued, Measure 1 was discontinued. Ships painted in Measure 1 would continue to carry the scheme, however, until repainting took place during overhaul or as the new paints became available.

Because the Measure 1 Dark Gray System was only to be eliminated as ships needed repainting or overhaul, or when the new paints were available, most of the Battle Force that had been relocated from San Pedro, California to Pear Harbor in the Territory of Hawaii was still painted in Dark Gray (5-D) when the Japanese naval and air forces attacked on 7 December 1941. Destroyers in Measure 1 in 1941 included the CASSIN (DD-372) and the SHAW (DD-372), both were severely damaged at Pearl Harbor, the WARRINGTON (DD-383) and SAMPSON (DD-384), as well as many of the BENSON (DD-421) Class vessels operating in the Pacific.

The NOA (DD-343) was camouflaged in Measure 1, the Dark Gray system, when it operated as a training ship at the U.S. Naval Academy, Annapolis, Maryland in 1941. Hull and superstructure were painted Dark Gray (5-D) and the stacks and foremast were painted Light Gray (5-L). The stacks have yet to be painted in the Dark Gray as required by the *Ships-2* directive. On the aft superstructure of the NOA is the aircraft-handling crane that was used to test the feasibility of carrying floatplanes on destroyers. (Elsilrac)

(Top) The CONYGHAM (DD-371), camouflaged in Measure 1, the Dark Gray System, pulls up alongside another destroyer to deliver guard mail and perhaps a movie. The CONYNGHAM has oversized bloomers fitted to the Number 1 and 2 gun mounts to keep the seawater from entering the mounts. All of the sailors on the forecastle are dressed in light uniforms; once the war began all hands were ordered into blue dress so as not to stand out on the deck. (U.S. Navy)

(Middle) The KANE (DD-235) is camouflaged in Measure 1, which required that all vertical and horizontal surfaces, except wood decks and masts, be painted Dark Gray. The fore and main mast are painted Light Gray as are the ready round lockers for the 4-inch (101.6 mm) ammunition. The KANE was sailing in Puget Sound, Washington on 8 February 1942 on her way to Todd Shipyards for conversion to High Speed Transport (APD). (Real War Photos)

(Bottom) The CHANDLER (DD-206/DMS-9) makes flank speed in a heavy cross sea in the Pacific, north of the Territory of Hawaii, on 7 December 1941 in a desperate search for the Japanese fleet. The tip of the stacks and the fore mast are painted Light Gray (5-L), while the rest of the ship is painted Dark Gray (5-D) (Real War Photos)

7

Measure 2, The Graded System

The second of the paint schemes introduced in January 1941 was Measure 2, the Graded System. The instructions under Measure 2 called for all vertical surfaces above the lowest deck edge sheer line, including stacks, masts, superstructures, and gun directors, to be painted Light Gray (5-L). The sides of the hull were to be painted in three bands, with the top being Light Gray (5-L), the middle band Ocean Gray (5-O), and the lowest band, the one closest to the water, Dark Gray (5-D). The decks and all horizontal surfaces, including sloping surfaces, were to be painted Dark Gray (5-D).

The idea behind the Measure 2 scheme was to make the ship appear farther away from the observer than it actually was. The Light Gray (5-L) would help the superstructure blend into the sky and the Dark Gray (5-D) of the hull would help to blend into the water. The scheme also provided some amount of course, range, and distance deception whether during the day or the night. The ship's pennant number was painted in black and situated on the upper hull side at the break in the sheer line.

Some of the BENSON Class (DD-421) would receive this camouflage scheme during 1941, with the GLEAVES (DD-423), NIBLAK (DD-424), LANSDALE (DD-426), MONSSEN (DD-436) and the LUDLOW (DD-438) painted in this design.

The CHARLES F. HUGHES (DD-428) rides at anchor camouflaged in Measure 2 paint scheme. The Light Gray (5-L) color has been painted over the rounded hull line to meet with the Dark Gray (5-D) deck paint. The HUGHES provided convoy duty in the Atlantic in 1942 camouflaged in this scheme. (Elsilrac)

The class leader BENSON (DD-421) sails out of Boston Navy Yard on 27 June 1941 in camouflage Measure 2, the Graded System. The hull number (421) is painted on the hull, just forward of the break in the sheer line. The colors used, in bands, from the water up, are Dark Gray (5-D), Ocean Gray (5-O) and Light Gray (5-L). Light Gray was painted on the superstructure, masts and all other vertical surfaces. The deck was painted in Dark Gray (5-D). (National Archives)

The GLEAVES (DD-423) rides at anchor camouflaged in Measure 2, the Graded System. The roofs of the Number 3 and 4 turrets have yet to be installed, as in her sister ship, BENSON. Measure 2 was authorized in the January 1941 edition of *Ships.* The Dark Gray (5-D) paint can be seen on the roofs of the turrets. (Floating Drydock)

Measure 3, The Light Gray System

Light Gray (5-L) was designated as Measure 3 in the January 1941 issue of *Ships-2*. The Light Gray System was the new nomenclature for what had been the Standard Navy Gray paint scheme, introduced in 1928.

In Measure 3, all vertical surfaces of the hull, sides of superstructure, stacks, and masts (including pole masts) were painted Light Gray (5-L). All horizontal surfaces, except wood decks, were painted Dark Gray (5-D). Wood decks stayed in natural, bleached wood color.

Measure 3 provided low visibility to surface observers in hazy and foggy conditions, although aerial observers noted increased visibility. The Light Gray scheme, along with the large, shaded hull numbers, were utilized until the start of WWII in the Atlantic and Pacific on a variety of ships not utilizing the other five measures authorized by *Ships-2*.

The BUCK (DD-420) is painted Standard Navy Gray, which would become Measure 3 in the January 1941 issue of *Ships-2*. DD-420's large, white shaded hull numbers would soon give way to 24-inch (60.9mm) unshaded numbers. (Floating Dry Dock)

Measure 4, The Black System

The Black System, introduced by *Ships-2* in January 1941, specified that all vertical surfaces, such as the sides of the hull, sides of superstructures, gun directors, and stacks, were to be painted Formula #82 Dull Black. Pole masts and vertical surfaces above the top of the stacks were to be painted Light Gray (5-L), however.

A Dark Gray (5-D) was the color for the horizontal surfaces other than wood decks. The wood decks were not to be darkened, pending further investigation. Sloping surfaces were to be painted in Dark Gray.

The Black System would have been uncomfortable in the hotter climes such as the Mid-Atlantic and the Pacific Area of Operation. It appears that very few destroyers were actually painted in Measure 4 during 1941. Personal accounts and photographic evidence indicate that the Destroyer Leaders DAVIS (DD-395) and SAMPSON (DD-394) as well as the CASE (DD-370) and SWANSON (DD-443) wore the Black scheme.

(Top) The DAVIS (DD-395) is getting its Measure 4, camouflaged scheme painted over with the Measure 14, the Ocean Gray System in 1942. The Black System offered some degree of protection during nighttime operations and certain other light conditions, but crew comfort suffered. Measure 4 utilized a dull black Number 82 paint. (Real War Photos)

(Bottom) The CASE (DD-370) was painted in Measure 4, the Black System, during experiments that took place at Pearl Harbor, Territory of Hawaii, during July and August 1940. The CASE was painted with a Black formula 82, a matte paint, with the masts painted Light Gray (5-L), and all horizontal surfaces, including the deck, painted Dark Gray (5-D). Following the experiments, in the January 1941 edition of *Ships-2*, Measure 4 received authorization. The Black exterior would have been extremely uncomfortable in hot tropical climates such as the South Pacific. When the next edition of *Ships-2* Revision 1 was printed, Measure 4 no longer appeared. (U.S. Navy Via Elsilrac)

Measure 5, Painted Bow Wave

Measure 5, the Painted Bow Wave, was the most elaborate of the early schemes authorized by the January 1941 edition of *Ships-2*. The desired effect was speed deception: making the ships appear to be moving much faster than they actually were.

The instructions called for the bow wave to be painted a Dark Blue or Green. If those colors were not available, Black or Dark Gray could be utilized. The edge of the white foam should start at the bow and arch upwards toward the sheer line and then move down the side of the hull in a wavy manner, so as to emulate water passing along on the side of the hull. The upper edge of the white foam should be fairly sharp, while the lower edge should be soft and blend with the darker color of the lower hull.

The Painted Bow Wave could be used with Measures 1, 2, or 3, but not with 4, the Black System, since there would not be enough of a color differential. Measure 5 was known to be worn by the ELLET (DD-398) and BAILEY (DD-492).

The BAILEY (DD-492) was camouflaged in Measure 5, the Painted Bow Wave, when photographed in December 1943. The false bow wave was painted in dark blue, green, or gray, outlined in white to simulate foam, and was utilized on Measures 1, 2, and 3, but not 4. Measure 5 had been authorized in January 1941 and discontinued in September 1941. The fact that the BAILEY wore the Measure 5 scheme in December 1943 makes this an instance in which official directives were ignored. (Real War Photos)

Measure 11, The Sea Blue System

Measures 6 through 10 applied only to cruisers (CA and CL) and to submarines (SS), so the next measure that was applicable to destroyers was Measure 11, the Sea Blue System.

Ships-2, Revised, issued on 1 September 1941, called for all vertical surfaces from the boot topping to the top of the superstructure masses, pole masts, yards, and various slender upper works above the level of top superstructures, to be painted Sea Blue (5-S). The directive also dictated that all horizontal surfaces, including the canvas covers and all decks, should be painted Deck Blue (20-B).

Members of the FARRAGUT (DD-348) Class and some members of the PORTER (DD-356) Class wore Measure 11 paint during 1941, prior to its replacement by Measure 12, the Graded System, or Measure 21, the Navy Blue System.

The PORTER (DD-356) was one of 13 of the "heavy" destroyer leaders of 1933-1935. She is camouflaged in Measure 11, the Sea Blue System, that was authorized in September 1941. The Sea Blue System called for all of the vertical surfaces, including the masts, to be painted Sea Blue (5-S) and horizontal surfaces to be painted Deck Blue (20-B). (Floating Dry Dock)

The Graded System, Measure 12 was authorized by *Ships-2, Revised,* on 1 September 1941. It called for the use of Sea Blue (5-S) from the boot topping to the highest level of the main deck or sheer line, with Ocean Gray (5-O) above that level. Pole masts and upper works were to be painted in Haze Gray (5-H). The deck and all horizontal surfaces, including canvas covers, were to be painted Deck Blue (20-B). Measure 12 was very similar to Measure 2, The Graded System, and it was soon abandoned in favor of Measure 12 Modified.

Measure 12 Modified (Mod) was the only measure for which the application was left up the yardmaster and painters. General direction and suggested applications were provided for the splotches and blotches of paint, but no definitive overall designs were provided.

The colors to be used were Sea Blue (5-S), Haze Gray (5-H), and Ocean Gray (5-O). and they were to be applied in irregular patterns or splotches, with either soft or hard edges. The directive called for the use of one or two colors of splotches over the basic painted surface of the ship, which was either the second or third color. Thus, if the main surface was Sea Blue (5-S), then the splotches were to be Ocean Gray (5-O) and/or Haze Gray or a combination of both. The directive specified that no exact form of splotches could or would be specified. Only one aspect of the directive that was to be a constant was the provision that all horizontal surfaces were to be Deck Blue (20-B).

Measure 12 Modified was utilized in both the Atlantic and Pacific during 1942 and every destroyer and destroyer escort wore a different scheme. There were two and perhaps more variants of the basic Measure 12 Modified designs. Measure 12 R Modified was a scheme that elongated the second and/or the third color along the hull line and appears to have been applied to the older CLEMSON (DD-186) Class of older destroyers.

The FARENHOLT (DD-491) carried a Measure 12 Modified scheme that was similar to the 12 R Mod that is thought to have used greens in a wavy pattern along the sides of the hull and on the stacks. The colors could never be verified and it will have to be assumed that the standard colors of 5-H, 5-S, and 5-O would have been utilized. The FARENHOLT was in the company of the fleet carrier WASP (CV-7) during August and September 1942 while she was operating in the area of the Solomons.

Measure 12 was the most highly interpreted of all of the measures utilized during WWII, but it was superseded by Measure 21, the Navy Blue System, by 1943. One can only imagine the ship's crews applying the camouflage paints, attempting to outdo other destroyers in the fleet as to design and application.

The MacLEISH (DD-220), a CLEMSON Class modified destroyer, was camouflaged in a Modified Measure 12 scheme in 1942. She is flying her recognition flags of N, U, P, T, from her yards. Only two colors appear to have been used, Haze Gray (5-H) and Sea Blue (5-S). The MacLEISH had been modified as an ocean escort with the removal of one boiler and one stack. (Floating Dry Dock)

The CORRY (DD-463) was camouflaged in Measure 12 Modified in 1942. The three colors used were Ocean Gray (5-O) as the basic hull and superstructure color with wavy bands of Haze Gray (5-H) and Sea Blue (5-S). The hull numbers are black. The CORRY sank the German U-801 in March 1944 and herself was sunk on D-Day 6 June 1944 off of Utah Beach, Normandy, France, when she struck a mine. She earned four Battle Stars for her service in the Atlantic. (Floating Dry Dock)

Camouflaged in a modified Measure 12, the LUDLOW (DD-438) moves off of Navy Yard, Boston, Massachusetts, in August 1942. She flies her recognition flags of N, E, T, and R at her yards. The basic hull color of Ocean Gray (5-O) was painted with wavy bands of Sea Blue (5-S) and Haze Gray (5-H). The LUDLOW earned six Battle Stars for her service in the Atlantic. (Floating Dry Dock)

The basic hull color on the BARTON (DD-599) was Sea Blue (5-S) with Ocean Gray (5-O) patches extending down over the sheer line. The superstructure is painted in Haze Gray (5-H), Sea Blue (5-S), and Ocean Gray (5-O). The deck and the tops of the gun mounts and director are Deck Blue (20-B). The BARTON was sunk off of Guadalcanal on 13 November 1942. (Floating Dry Dock)

Another example of Measure 12, Modified, was applied to the WAINWRIGHT (DD-419), sailing off of Navy Yard, Norfolk, Virginia, in March 1942. The basic hull color is Ocean Gray (5-O) with panels of Sea Blue (5-S) on the hull, and Haze Gray (5-H) and Ocean Gray (5-O) on the superstructure and gun mounts. The radar antennas have yet to be fitted. DD-419 was commissioned in 15 April 1940. For its WWII service, the WAINWRIGHT earned seven Battle Stars. (Floating Dry Dock)

The basic hull color on the BARTON (DD-599) was Sea Blue (5-S) with Ocean Gray (5-O) patches extending down over the sheer line. The superstructure is painted in Haze Gray (5-H), Sea Blue (5-S) and Ocean Gray (5-O). The deck and the tops of the gun mounts and director are Deck Blue (20-B). The BARTON was sunk off of Guadalcanal on 13 November 1942. (Floating Dry Dock)

The FARENHOLT (DD-491) was camouflaged in this unusual and singular example of Measure 12 modified in 1942 when she operated in the Pacific. The camouflage scheme showed strong British influence with its use of elongated patterns of Ocean Gray (5-O) and Haze Gray (5-H) on a basic hull and superstructure color of Sea Blue (5-S). The wartime censors have removed the radar antennas on the foremast. (Floating Dry Dock)

Measure 13, Haze Gray System

Measure 13, the Haze Gray System, was authorized by *Ships-2 Revised,* on 1 September 1941. It called for all vertical surfaces from the boot-topping to the top of the masts on the ship to be painted Haze Gray (5-H). All the horizontal surfaces, including canvas covers, were to be painted Deck Blue (20-B). This measure provided excellent protection during foggy or inclement weather. On the other hand, it resulted in higher-than-normal visibility during daylight or moonlit times.

Measure 13 was little used in 1942, as ship commanders preferred a multi-color camouflage scheme, such as Measure 12 Modified, believing that it provided a degree of concealment and also boosted crew moral.

When the war ended in 1945, the Atlantic and Pacific Fleets began a massive repainting program, over-painting Measure 21 and 22 in favor of Measure 13, which was soon to be renamed Measure 27, a measure that is presently being utilized by the U.S. Navy.

The STANLY (DD-478) undergoes a camouflage change from Measure 21, the Navy Blue System to Measure 13, the Haze Gray System, following the end of Word War II. Measure 13 employed Haze Gray (5-H) over all vertical surfaces, and Deck Blue (20-B) on all horizontal surfaces. Measure 13 would be designated Measure 27, the "peace time gray" camouflage scheme that is still utilized on U.S. Navy warships in the 21st century. (Floating Dry Dock)

Measure 14, Ocean Gray System

Measure 14, the Ocean Gray System, was authorized by *Ships-2, Revised* on 1 September 1941. It specified that all vertical surfaces from the boot topping to the top of the superstructure were to be painted with Ocean Gray (5-O), and all pole masts, yards, and slender upper works with Haze Gray (5-H). All horizontal surfaces, including canvas covers, were to be painted or stained Deck Blue (20-B). Measure 14 provided low visibility to surface observers in daylight, but it provided high visibility to aerial observers.

As with Measure 13, Measure 14 was little used on destroyers or destroyer escorts. When they had a choice, skippers preferred a camouflage scheme that they thought would give some degree of concealment. Measure 14 was discontinued with the March 1943 revision of *Ships-2*, since the Bureau of Ships felt that the Measure 31-33 schemes offered better concealment.

(Above) The KENNISON (DD-138) sails between an "R" Class submarine in Measure 9 and a FLETCHER Class destroyer camouflaged in Measure 31/23d in this June 1944 photo. The KENNISON must have just been through a yard period as the stack deflectors have been removed, new stack extensions have been added, and the weather screen has been removed from the searchlight platform. (Real War Photos)

(Opposite Page) The KENNISON (DD-138) carries Measure 14, the Ocean Gray System, in this February 1944 photo. Measure 14 called for all vertical surfaces to be painted in Ocean Gray, with all horizontal surfaces to be painted in Deck Blue (20-B). The combing on the underside of the bridge area has also been painted Deck Blue. The KENNISON, a WICKES Class destroyer, has been converted to an ocean escort with the removal of one boiler and one stack. (Real War Photos)

Mountbatten Pink

The use of Mountbatten Pink, a British Admiralty color, on U.S. Navy destroyers came about quite by accident in December 1941. The WINSLOW (DD-359) was traversing from the Pacific to the Atlantic and had made a port call at Cape Town, South Africa, for resupply and some rest and recreation (R & R) for the crew. Her Sapphire Blue, Measure 1B was in need of repainting and the captain was told of the concealment value of Mountbatten Pink.

Lord Louis Mountbatten, who commanded a flotilla of British destroyers, discovered the concealment value of Mountbatten Pink and had his ships so painted. The gray lavender paint for the WINSLOW had been procured from the stocks of the Dunotter Castle, a ship in the Union-Castle Line. The paint was the official color of the shipping line.

Once the painting of the WINSLOW was completed, she sailed for her scheduled refit in New York. While in transit, other U.S. Navy destroyers observed the WINSLOW, and the captains commented on the camouflage effect of the Mountbatten Pink paint. Other destroyers that were operating in the Mid-Atlantic and were also repainted from their Measure 12R Modified Graded System to the Mountbatten Pink were the WARRINGTON (DD-383), CLARK (DD-361), and PHELPS (DD-360) - all Flagships of their respective Destroyer Squadrons.

The Mountbatten Pink paint was applied on all vertical and horizontal surfaces on U.S. Navy destroyers. No official number was given to the paint and instead it was unofficially known as Mountbatten Pink (Dark). U.S. Navy sailors affectionately called the color "nipple pink," while the British called it Plymouth Pink

Mountbatten Pink was carried by a few U.S. destroyers into early 1943, when both the Atlantic and Pacific fleets began repainting most ships in Navy Blue (5-N), Measure 21.

The PHELPS (DD-360), a few other "destroyer leaders," and destroyers that were operating in the Atlantic in 1942 and 1943 were camouflaged in Mountbatten Pink. Lord Louis Mountbatten had discovered the camouflage properties of the purple-gray paint that was the official color of the Union-Castle Shipping Line. The lavender color paint provided good concealment at dawn and dusk, times when German U-Boat commanders liked to hunt. Mountbatten Pink was applied to all vertical and horizontal surfaces on the vessel. (Floating Dry Dock)

Measure 15, Disruption System

Measure 15, the Disruption System, was conceived from Anti-Submarine Warfare (ASW) British Admiralty schemes that were being utilized in the Atlantic. The Disruption System was not an official scheme and it was applied to only three U.S. Navy ships, the battleship INDIANA (BB-58), the tanker TALLULAH (AO-50), and the destroyer HOBSON (DD-464).

Since Measure 15 was not an official scheme, the colors used are speculative and were likely White (5-U), Haze Gray (5-H), Sea Blue (5-S), and Light Gray (5-L), with the deck painted in Deck Blue (20-B). The June 1942 issue of *Ships–2* made no mention of Measure 15, further relegating the measure to speculation. The design appears to have been applied to all three of the ships in the same manner and the pattern was the same on both sides.

Measure 15 appears to have influenced the later Measures 31 and 32 schemes, which employed multiple colors in geometric patterns. No instructions for painting the deck were mentioned in any publication, but one can surmise that Deck Blue (20-B) would have been used.

A camouflage design that traced its origins to a British Anti-Submarine Warfare scheme, Measure 15, the Disruption System, was applied to the HOBSON (DD-464) in the summer of 1942. The colors are speculative and might have been White (5-U), Haze Gray (5-H), Sea Blue (5-S), and Light Gray (5-L). Measure 15 was painted the same on both starboard and port sides. Measures 31 through 33 appear to have developed out of Measure 15. (Real War Photos)

Measure 16, Thayer System

The Thayer System, sometimes called the Thayer Blue System, employed the color known as Thayer Blue (5-B), a hue developed by naturalist Abbot H. Thayer. Thayer was a painter who specialized in the natural concealment value of the colors on animals and birds, and was an early pioneer in the use of white paint on ships.

British artist and naturalist Peter Scott, who had provided paint designs to the Admiralty during WWI, was an advocate of the use of white on ships. His designs were employed in a scheme designated as Western Approaches and used mainly in the North Atlantic during WWII. The U.S. Navy saw the value of white ships in that rainy, cold, and foggy environment and adopted a design and color choice for use in the North Atlantic. Thayer's design employed White (5-U) and Thayer Blue (5-B)

The design was different on each side, and the only reason that blue was added to the design was in case the ship happened to be seen in sunny weather. Photographs of Measure 16 prove the point, as the ships appear to glow in the sunshine. The panels of Thayer Blue were applied on the overall ship's color of White (5-U). The deck and all horizontal surfaces, including canvas covers were to be painted or stained Deck Blue (20-B). Thayer Blue was made by adding one pint of 5-BTM Blue (a blue tinting material) to 40 pints of White. Thus the blue was extremely light in nature and in fact on moonlit nights the blue could not be discerned at distance.

Thayer Blue made its appearance in 1943 and destroyers known to employ Measure 16 were the WARRINGTON (DD-383), SAMPSON (DD-394), and DAVIS (DD-395).

The Thayer System seems to have had an influence on the later Measure 31, the Dark Pattern System; 32, the Medium Pattern System; and 33, the Light Pattern System.

The SAMPSON (DD-394) is camouflaged in Measure 16, the Thayer Blue System, as she sails in the Gulf of Panama in March 1943. Artist and naturalist Abbot H. Thayer developed the scheme that employed White (5-U) and Thayer Blue (5-B). The design featured an overall white ship with panels of the pale Thayer Blue. Only the 4 in the ship's hull number of 394 has been painted in light blue on the forward hull. (Real War Photos)

The SAMPSON operates out of her element in the Gulf of Panama in March 1943. The camouflage system of Thayer Blue was designed for use in the North Atlantic where foggy and rainy conditions exist, contrary to the sunny climes of Central American waters. The SAMPSON was transiting from the Pacific to the Atlantic Ocean via the Panama Canal to continue convoy escort duties following an overhaul. (Real War Photos)

An aerial oblique port side view shows the SAMPSON (DD-394) operating in the Gulf of Panama in 1943. The deck, gun mount and gun director tops and other horizontal surfaces are painted in Deck Blue. In full sunlight, the pale Thayer Blue paint is so light that it appears white. The Thayer Blue System enjoyed great success in the rainy and foggy conditions of the North Atlantic. (Real War Photos)

In cloudy foggy weather the pale Thayer Blue (5-B) shows up quite well on the port side of the WARRINGTON (DD-383) in this 1943 photograph. The engineer has just cleaned the stack by blowing steam. What appears to be a silhouette of a penguin has been painted on the stack. The Deck Blue (20-B) paint has been painted down over the sides of all three-gun mounts. (Floating Dry Dock)

The Navy Blue System, Measure 21, first appeared in the June 1942 issue of *Ships-2* and was an outgrowth of the Measure 11, Sea Blue System, that utilized a lighter shade of blue.

The June 1942 directive called for all vertical surfaces on the ship without exception to be painted in Navy Blue (5-N), and all horizontal surfaces, including canvas covers, to be painted or stained in Deck Blue (20-B). The Navy Blue provided the lowest measure of visibility to aerial observers during day, night, or searchlight conditions. The Navy Blue was highly visible to surface observers, but it did provide some deception as to course and speed. This Measure was soon applied to many destroyers in all war zones.

Measure 21 would be employed during 1943 and early 1944 until it was replaced by the geometric designs (Measures 31-33) that came into vogue in 1944. It is perhaps interesting that when the kamikaze attacks began in earnest in 1944 the U.S. Navy began to paint over the "dazzle" designs with Navy Blue (5-N) or Measure 22, the Graded System paint schemes designed to reduce aerial observance.

Measure 21 was utilized until the end of WWII when Measure 13 was painted over the Navy Blue. Measure 13 would then soon be designated "Measure 27" also known as "peace time gray."

The FOX (DD-234), a CLEMSON Class destroyer, was camouflaged in Measure 21, the Navy Blue System, in September 1943. Measure 21 called for the ship's vertical surfaces to be Navy Blue (5-N) and all horizontal surfaces to be Deck Blue (20-B). The white circle at the base of the Number 1 gun mount on the deck indicated the operating area of the gun barrel. The FOX had been converted to an ocean escort by removing one boiler and one stack. (Real War Photos)

The destroyer escort ENGLAND (DE-635) was one of the most highly-decorated destroyers of WWII, earning a Presidential Unit Citation for sinking six Japanese submarines. The ENGLAND is seen here camouflaged in a well-worn Measure 21. On 9 May 1945, a Japanese kamikaze slammed into the ENGLAND off Okinawa, damaging her so severely that her conversion to High Speed Transport (APD) was cancelled. (Floating Dry Dock)

The NICHOLSON (DD-442) was camouflaged in Measure 21 when she sailed out of Navy Yard, New York on 8 January 1944. She appears to have some damage to her forward hull below the Number One gun mount. The NICHOLSON was awarded 10 Battle Stars for her service in the Atlantic and Pacific. The canvas sheeting above the bridge and on the 20mm gun mounts has been stained, per the *Ships-2* directive, in Deck Blue. (Floating Dry Dock)

Coming up along side the escort carrier MANILA (CVE-61) during operations in the Pacific in February 1944, the CALDWELL (DD-605) prepares to take men on board. The CALDWELL is camouflaged in Measure 21 with all canvas covers stained Deck Blue (20-B). Hit by a Japanese kamikaze on 12 December 1944, CALDWELL earned eight Battle Stars for her service in the Pacific. (Real War Photos)

The GANSEVOORT (DD-608), shown here in 1944, appears in freshly-applied Measure 21 that was over painted from Measure 22, the Graded System. A kamikaze struck the GANSEVOORT on 30 December 1944, knocking her out of action for the rest of the war. She earned four Battle Stars for her service in the Pacific. (Floating Dry Dock)

The STANLY (DD-478) follows closely in the wake of another ship as they both sail out of a harbor in the Pacific on 23 March 1944. She is camouflaged in Measure 21 and her recognition signal flags fly from the yards. Sailors man the starboard rails in a sign of respect as she passes the light cruiser MONTPELIER (CL-57). (Real War Photos)

The LAVALLETTE (DD-448) sails out of San Diego Harbor past an oiler (AO) in 1945. She had her Measure 31/24d scheme over painted with Navy Blue (5-N) for service in the Pacific. Measure 21 was found to offer greater protection from Japanese kamikaze attacks that became prevalent beginning in 1944. All of the hatches on the 5-inch gun mounts are open to increase ventilation. (Floating Dry Dock)

The NICHOLAS (DD-449) wears a fresh coat of Navy Blue (5-N) paint in 1945, covering her Measure 31/24d, Dark Pattern camouflage that had been applied in 1944. The significance of her hull number appearing twice is unknown. The black boot topping has not been applied in a straight line as specified. (Floating Dry Dock)

The HUGH PURVIS (DD-709) sails out Federal Shipbuilding and Drydock in Kearny, New Jersey, on 28 February 1945. She is camouflaged in Measure 21, the Navy Blue System, on her acceptance trials. Various civilians from the shipbuilders company are present on the forecastle on this cold winter day. (Floating Dry Dock)

The DeHAVEN (DD-727) is tied up to a mooring point in 1945 camouflaged in Measure 21, the Navy Blue System. The ALLEN M. SUMNER Class destroyer operated with Task Force 38 and 58 in the Pacific during WWII. She earned 11 Battle Stars for her flag for service in WWII and Korea, in addition to earning a Navy Unit Citation. (Real War Photos)

The GRAYSON (DD-435) was camouflaged in Measure 1, the Dark Gray System, in April 1941. The colors used were Dark Gray (5-D) on all vertical surfaces, with the pole masts, above the stacks, and gun director painted Light Gray (5-L). The deck was painted Dark Gray.

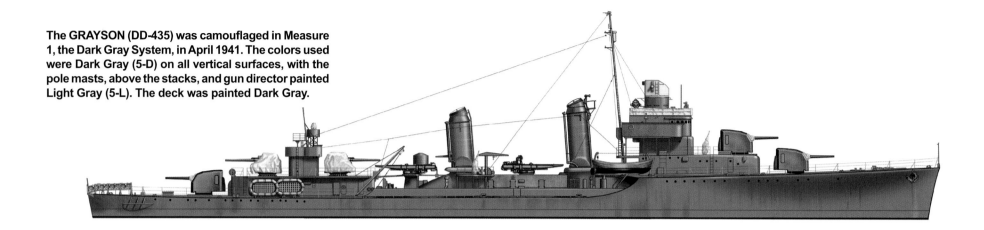

The GLEAVES (DD-423) carried camouflage Measure 2, the Graded System, in 1941. The colors used, from the Black Boot topping up, were Dark Gray (5-D), Ocean Gray (5-O), and Light Gray (5-L) on the balance of the vertical surfaces. The bands were to be parallel to the sea surface. The deck was to be painted Dark Gray (5-D). The pennant number was placed on the side of the hull in Black just below the bridge area.

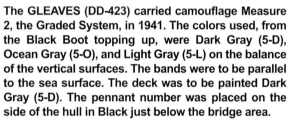

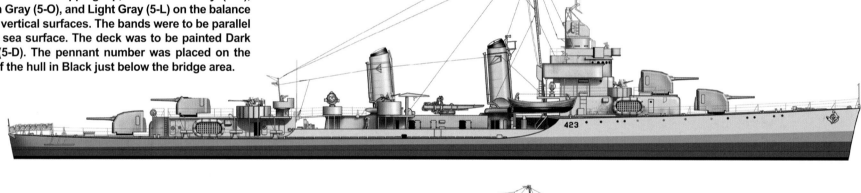

The ERRICSSON (DD-440) was painted in Measure 3, the Light Gray System, in 1941. The color used was Light Gray (5-L), also called Standard Navy Gray, with the deck painted in Dark Gray (5-D).

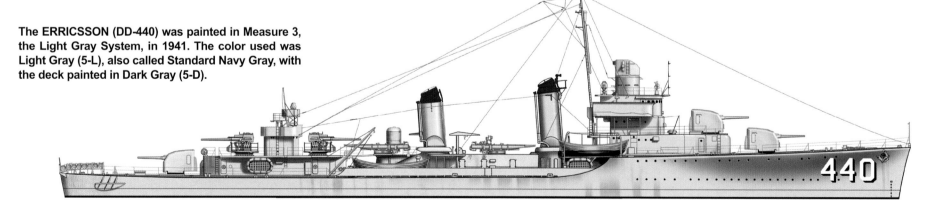

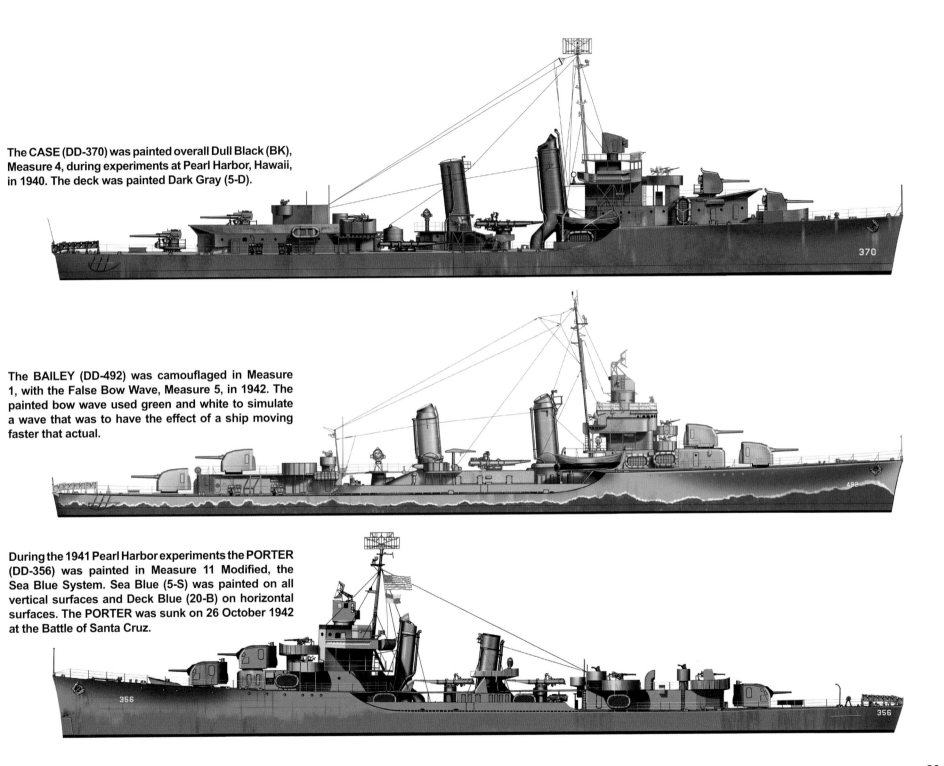

The CASE (DD-370) was painted overall Dull Black (BK), Measure 4, during experiments at Pearl Harbor, Hawaii, in 1940. The deck was painted Dark Gray (5-D).

The BAILEY (DD-492) was camouflaged in Measure 1, with the False Bow Wave, Measure 5, in 1942. The painted bow wave used green and white to simulate a wave that was to have the effect of a ship moving faster that actual.

During the 1941 Pearl Harbor experiments the PORTER (DD-356) was painted in Measure 11 Modified, the Sea Blue System. Sea Blue (5-S) was painted on all vertical surfaces and Deck Blue (20-B) on horizontal surfaces. The PORTER was sunk on 26 October 1942 at the Battle of Santa Cruz.

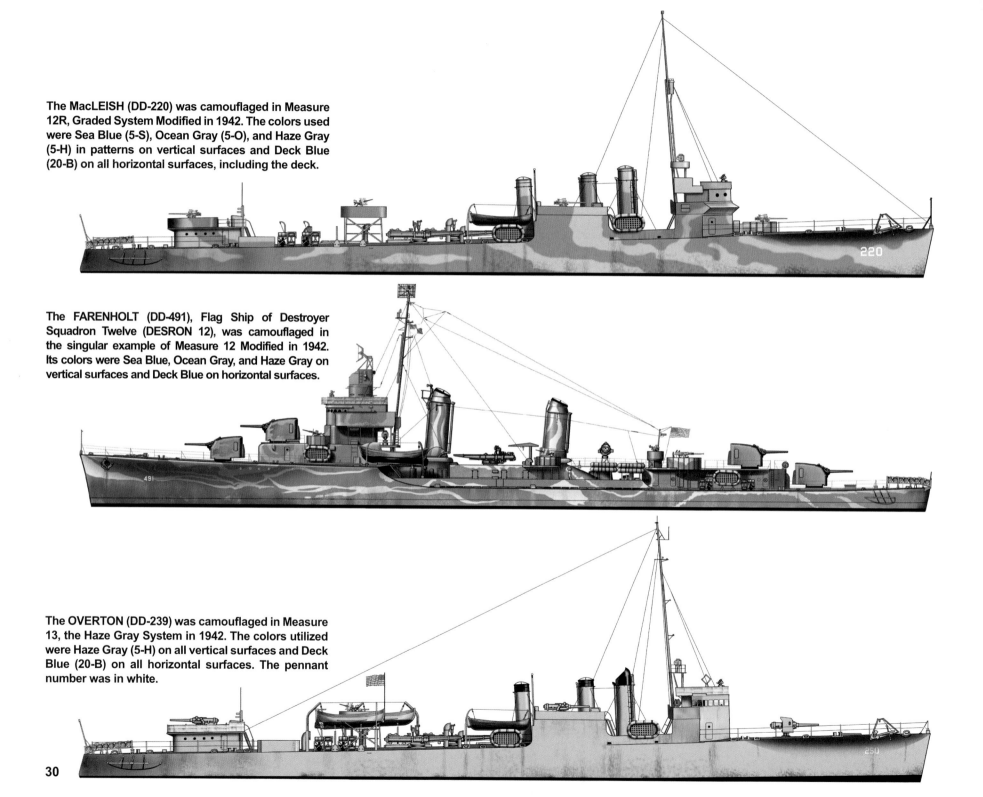

The MacLEISH (DD-220) was camouflaged in Measure 12R, Graded System Modified in 1942. The colors used were Sea Blue (5-S), Ocean Gray (5-O), and Haze Gray (5-H) in patterns on vertical surfaces and Deck Blue (20-B) on all horizontal surfaces, including the deck.

The FARENHOLT (DD-491), Flag Ship of Destroyer Squadron Twelve (DESRON 12), was camouflaged in the singular example of Measure 12 Modified in 1942. Its colors were Sea Blue, Ocean Gray, and Haze Gray on vertical surfaces and Deck Blue on horizontal surfaces.

The OVERTON (DD-239) was camouflaged in Measure 13, the Haze Gray System in 1942. The colors utilized were Haze Gray (5-H) on all vertical surfaces and Deck Blue (20-B) on all horizontal surfaces. The pennant number was in white.

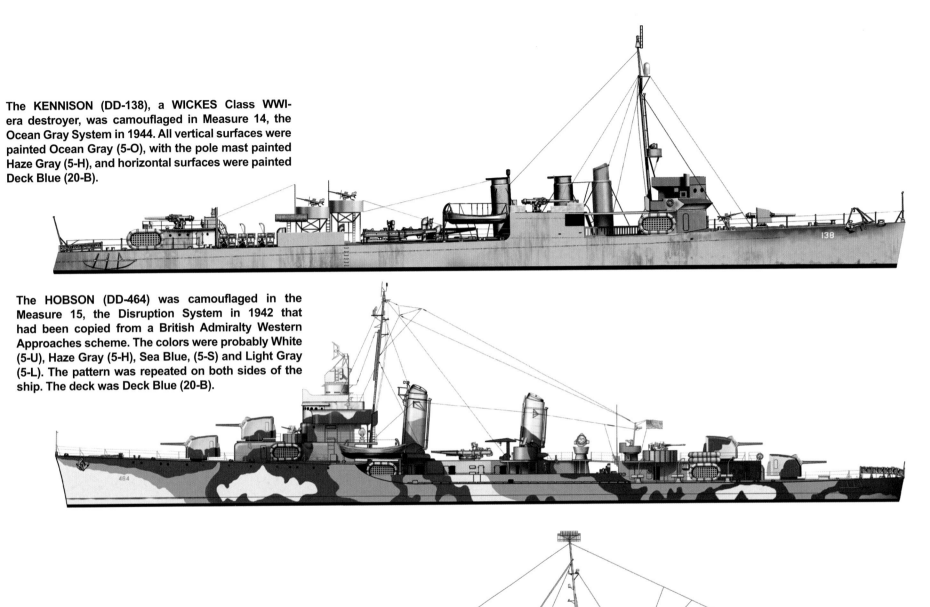

The KENNISON (DD-138), a WICKES Class WWI-era destroyer, was camouflaged in Measure 14, the Ocean Gray System in 1944. All vertical surfaces were painted Ocean Gray (5-O), with the pole mast painted Haze Gray (5-H), and horizontal surfaces were painted Deck Blue (20-B).

The HOBSON (DD-464) was camouflaged in the Measure 15, the Disruption System in 1942 that had been copied from a British Admiralty Western Approaches scheme. The colors were probably White (5-U), Haze Gray (5-H), Sea Blue, (5-S) and Light Gray (5-L). The pattern was repeated on both sides of the ship. The deck was Deck Blue (20-B).

The SAMPSON (DD-394) was camouflaged in Measure 16, the Thayer Blue System, in 1943/1944. The colors, which were suited to operations in the North Atlantic, were Thayer Blue (5-B) and White (5-U) on vertical surfaces and Deck Blue (20-B) on the deck and horizontal surfaces.

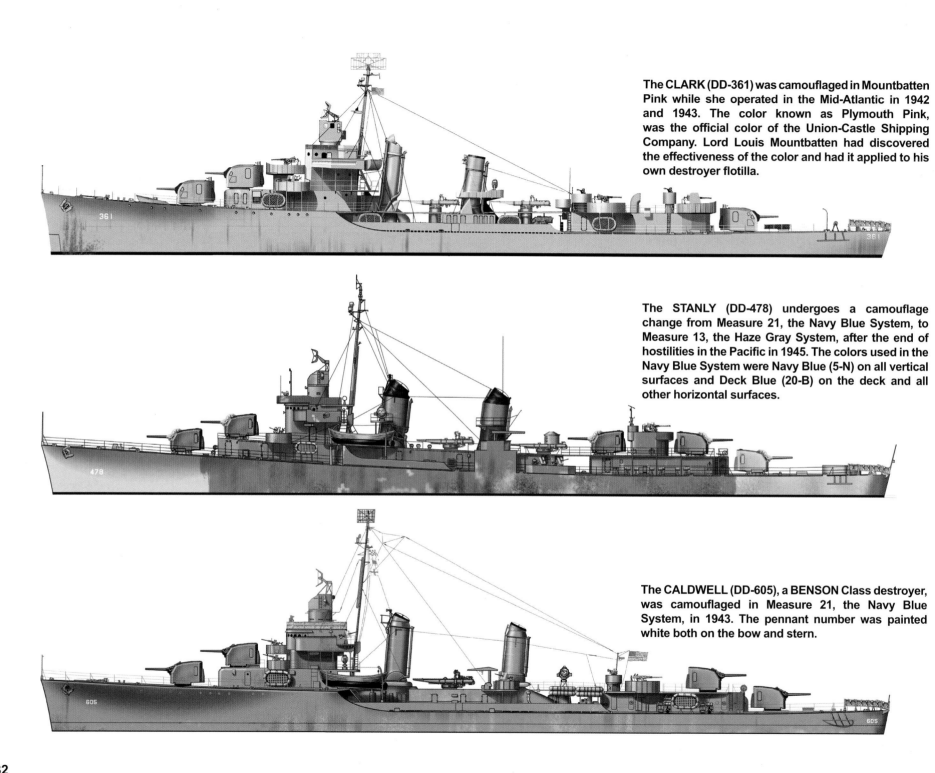

The CLARK (DD-361) was camouflaged in Mountbatten Pink while she operated in the Mid-Atlantic in 1942 and 1943. The color known as Plymouth Pink, was the official color of the Union-Castle Shipping Company. Lord Louis Mountbatten had discovered the effectiveness of the color and had it applied to his own destroyer flotilla.

The STANLY (DD-478) undergoes a camouflage change from Measure 21, the Navy Blue System, to Measure 13, the Haze Gray System, after the end of hostilities in the Pacific in 1945. The colors used in the Navy Blue System were Navy Blue (5-N) on all vertical surfaces and Deck Blue (20-B) on the deck and all other horizontal surfaces.

The CALDWELL (DD-605), a BENSON Class destroyer, was camouflaged in Measure 21, the Navy Blue System, in 1943. The pennant number was painted white both on the bow and stern.

Measure 22, The Graded System

The June 1942 issue of *Ships-2* authorized the use of Measure 22, the Graded System. Measure 22 was an outgrowth of Measure 2, also called the Graded System. Where Measure 2 used three colors, Measure 22 used only two—the newly-authorized purple blues and grays.

The directive called for painting the hull of the ship, from the boot topping up to the lowest point of the main deck, in Navy Blue (5-N), in a line that should parallel the waterline in a horizontal plane. Above the Navy Blue all remaining vertical surfaces including masts, yards and other gear were to be painted Haze Gray (5-H). Overhanging areas of the superstructure, such as gun tubs and bridge areas, were to be counter shaded on the undersides with White (5-U). The deck and all horizontal surfaces, including tops of gun mounts and canvas covers were to be painted or stained Deck Blue (20-B).

Measure 22 was first used in 1943 and, like Measure 21, was replaced, for the most part on destroyers, with the geometric designs in 1944. Destroyers would have been painted in 1943 or 1945 with either Measure 21 or 22. Destroyer Squadron commanders preferred that all the ships in the squadron or division be camouflaged in the same measure. This served the purpose of recognition degradation by the enemy and could cause an enemy to misidentify the type of ship under observation. As with Measure 21, following the end of WWII, destroyers painted in Measure 22 were soon over painted with Measure 13. Some destroyers, though, were observed still wearing Measure 22 in the Atlantic as late as 1949.

(Top Left) The "flush deck" destroyer, ocean escort LEARY (DD-158) is operating in the Atlantic four days before the German U-275 launched the Gnat torpedo that sank her on 24 December 1943. The LEARY is camouflaged in Measure 22, the Graded System, that was authorized in the June 1942 issue of *Ships-2 Revised.* The colors specified were Navy Blue (5-N) on the hull from the boot topping to the main deck edge at its lowest level, with the upper edge of the Navy Blue horizontal with the sea surface. All remaining vertical surfaces were to be painted Haze Gray (5-H). (Real War Photos)

(Bottom Left) The HARMON (DE-678) is camouflaged in Measure 22 in 1944. The HARMON was one of 10 BUCKLEY Class destroyers to have her open-mount 3-inch guns replaced by enclosed 5-inch mounts. The Navy Blue (5-N) paint line separating the Haze Gray (5-H) paint line does not follow a horizontal line as required by the *Ships-2* directive. The hull number 678 is in white. (Floating Dry Dock)

(Below) Four colors are visible on the hull of the SOLAR (DE-221), camouflaged in Measure 22. Red oxide paint extends up to the black boot topping, above that is the Navy Blue and Haze Gray. The SOLAR is equipped to hunt submarines in the Atlantic, with hedgehogs and a Huff/Duff (HF/DF) antenna fitted to the main mast. The SOLAR was lost on 30 April 1946 due to an internal explosion. Fenders have been placed over the side to protect the hull from scrapping damage. (Floating Dry Dock)

The **STRICKLAND** (DE-333) moves off of Navy Yard, New York on 15 March 1944 camouflaged in Measure 22. A white and red flag flies from the halyard indicating that the ship has a pilot onboard. The STRICKLAND, like most other destroyer escorts, is fitted out to hunt enemy submarines and to perform escort duties for convoys. (Floating Dry Dock)

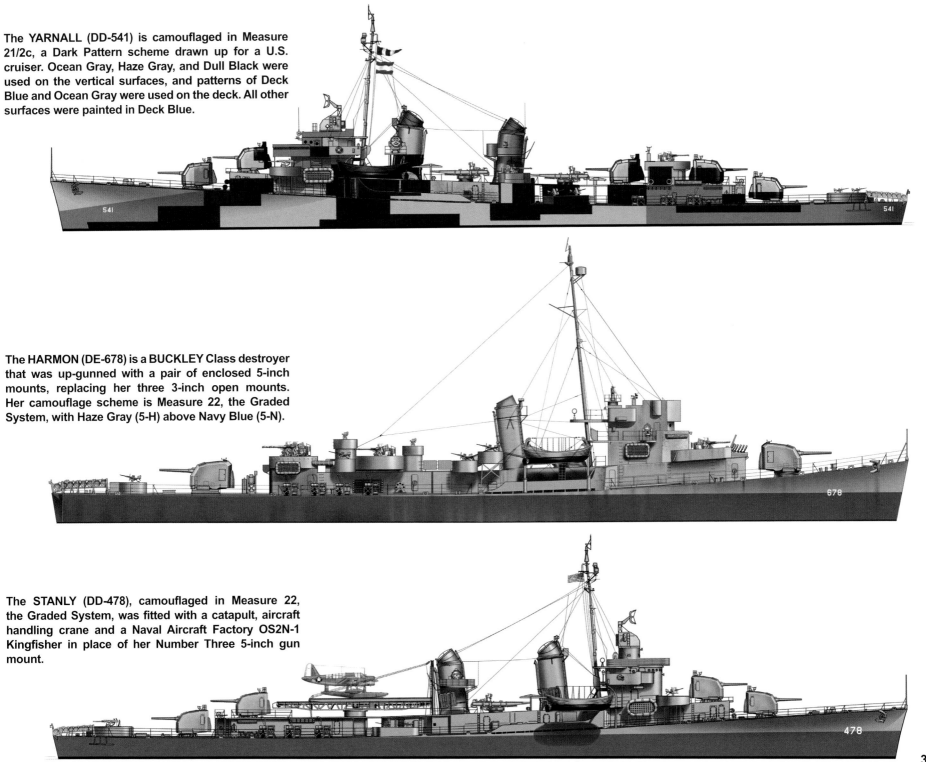

The YARNALL (DD-541) is camouflaged in Measure 21/2c, a Dark Pattern scheme drawn up for a U.S. cruiser. Ocean Gray, Haze Gray, and Dull Black were used on the vertical surfaces, and patterns of Deck Blue and Ocean Gray were used on the deck. All other surfaces were painted in Deck Blue.

The HARMON (DE-678) is a BUCKLEY Class destroyer that was up-gunned with a pair of enclosed 5-inch mounts, replacing her three 3-inch open mounts. Her camouflage scheme is Measure 22, the Graded System, with Haze Gray (5-H) above Navy Blue (5-N).

The STANLY (DD-478), camouflaged in Measure 22, the Graded System, was fitted with a catapult, aircraft handling crane and a Naval Aircraft Factory OS2N-1 Kingfisher in place of her Number Three 5-inch gun mount.

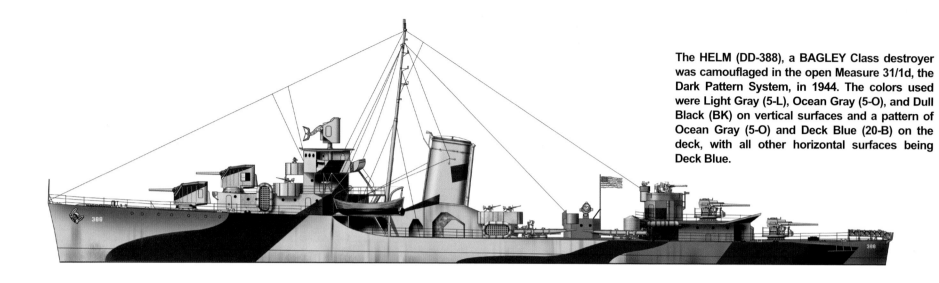

The HELM (DD-388), a BAGLEY Class destroyer was camouflaged in the open Measure 31/1d, the Dark Pattern System, in 1944. The colors used were Light Gray (5-L), Ocean Gray (5-O), and Dull Black (BK) on vertical surfaces and a pattern of Ocean Gray (5-O) and Deck Blue (20-B) on the deck, with all other horizontal surfaces being Deck Blue.

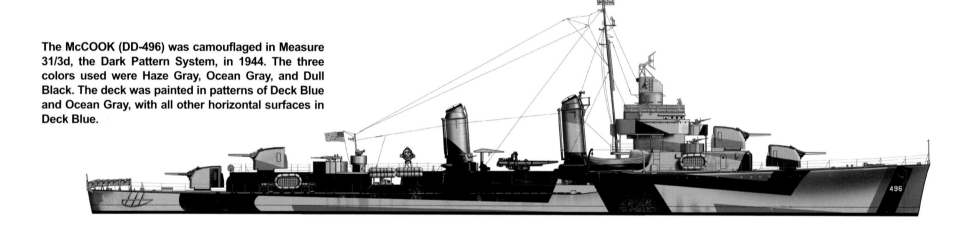

The McCOOK (DD-496) was camouflaged in Measure 31/3d, the Dark Pattern System, in 1944. The three colors used were Haze Gray, Ocean Gray, and Dull Black. The deck was painted in patterns of Deck Blue and Ocean Gray, with all other horizontal surfaces in Deck Blue.

The DALE (DD-353), a FARRAGUT Class destroyer, was camouflaged in Measure 31/6d, the Dark Pattern System, in 1944. The colors used were Ocean Gray, Haze Gray, and Dull Black on vertical surfaces and Deck Blue and Ocean Gray, in patterns on the deck, with all other horizontal surfaces being Deck Blue.

The FARRAGUT (DD-348), the lead ship of a new class of modern destroyers, was camouflaged in Measure 31/7d, the Dark Pattern System, in 1944. The two colors used on all vertical surfaces were Ocean Gray and Dull Black. The deck was painted in patterns of Deck Blue and Ocean Gray.

The BOYD (DD-544), a FLETCHER Class destroyer was camouflaged in the open Measure 31/10d, the Dark Pattern scheme. The two colors used were Dull Black and Ocean Gray on all vertical surfaces and Ocean Gray and Deck Blue in patterns on the deck. All other surfaces were painted Deck Blue.

The HAYNSWORTH (DD-700), an ALLEN M. SUMNER Class destroyer, was camouflaged in the open Measure 31/16d, the Dark Pattern System, derived somewhat from Measure 16, the Thayer Blue System. Measure 31/16d could also be adapted to BALTIMORE Class cruisers and CALIFORNIA Class battleships.

The CUMMINS (DD-365), a MAHAN Class destroyer, was camouflaged in Measure 31/23d, the Dark Pattern System, in 1944. Measure 31/23d used Ocean Gray, Haze Gray, and Dull Black on vertical surfaces and patterns of Deck Blue and Ocean Gray on the deck, with all other horizontal surfaces painted in Deck Blue.

The RINGGOLD (DD-500), a FLETCHER Class destroyer, was camouflaged in Measure 31/21d, the Dark Pattern System. The two-color scheme employed Ocean Gray and Dull Black on vertical surfaces, patterns of Deck Blue and Ocean Gray on the deck, and Deck blue on all other horizontal surfaces.

The HOWORTH (DD-592), a FLETCHER Class destroyer, was camouflaged in the two-color scheme of Measure 31/22d. Ocean Gray and Dull Black were painted on all vertical surfaces, and the deck was painted in patterns of Ocean Gray and Deck Blue, with all other horizontal surfaces painted Deck Blue.

The STANLY (DD-478) was one of six FLETCHER Class destroyers modified to carry a Kingfisher floatplane. The STANLY is camouflaged in Measure 22, and the floatplane is in the tri-color scheme adopted by the U.S. Navy in 1943. The floatplane addition required the removal of the Number three 5-inch gun mount. (U.S. National Archives)

The SURBRICK (DD-639), camouflaged in Measure 22, was photographed off Navy Yard, Portsmouth, Virginia on 31 March 1943, while preparing for a shake down cruise prior to joining the Atlantic Fleet. The SURBRICK served in the Atlantic, the Mediterranean, where she sustained bomb damage, and in the Pacific, where she was severely damaged by a Japanese kamikaze off Okinawa on 29 May 1945. (Floating Dry Dock)

The HARDING (DD-625) was camouflaged in Measure 22 in 1943 and soon joined the Atlantic Fleet. The HARDING participated in the Invasion of Normandy in June of 1944. She then assisted in the Invasion of Southern France in August 1944. She was then converted to a Destroyer Mine Sweeper (DMS) and reported to the Pacific. The HARDING earned four Battle Stars for her service. (Floating Dry Dock)

The GEARING (DD-710) was the lead ship in a class of large destroyers that became available in 1945. The GEARING, seen here alongside a staging wharf, is camouflaged in Measure 22. It is undergoing inclining tests at Federal Shipbuilding and Dry Dock on 25 April 1945. She was commissioned too late to see action in WWII. (Floating Dry Dock)

The RHIND (DD-404) wore Measure 22 while operating in the Pacific during 1945. She operated in the Atlantic for the majority of her career wearing Measure 12, Modified in 1942, Measure 22 in 1943 and 1945, and Measure 32/3d in 1944. She earned four Battle Stars for her service. The ship's whaleboat appears to be painted Navy Blue (5-N). Wartime censors have removed her SA air search radar from atop the foremast. (Floating Dry Dock)

The ALLEN M. SUMNER (DD-692) was the lead ship in a new class of destroyers that fitted six 5-inch guns in three mounts. She is pictured here in April 1945, camouflaged in Measure 22, a scheme that had just been painted over the earlier Measure 32/9d, which she carried in 1944. The ALLEN M. SUMNER saw service in both the Atlantic and Pacific during WWII, earning two Battle Stars. In the Korean War, she earned one Battle Star. In the War in Vietnam, she earned two Battle Stars. (Floating Dry Dock)

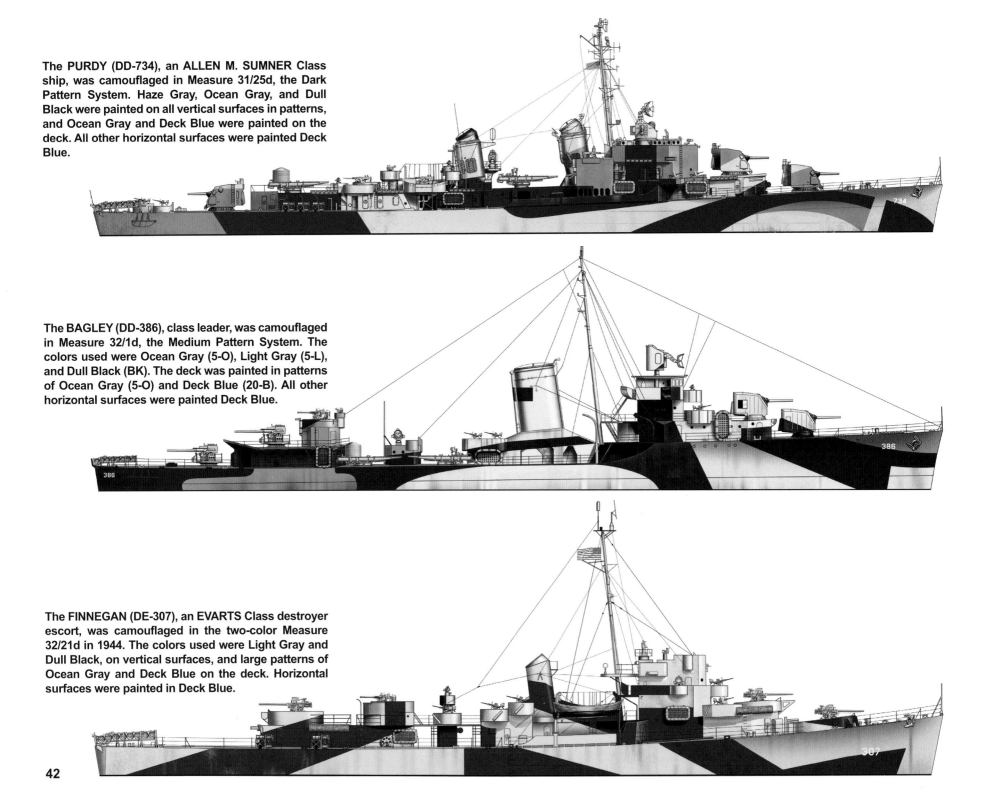

The PURDY (DD-734), an ALLEN M. SUMNER Class ship, was camouflaged in Measure 31/25d, the Dark Pattern System. Haze Gray, Ocean Gray, and Dull Black were painted on all vertical surfaces in patterns, and Ocean Gray and Deck Blue were painted on the deck. All other horizontal surfaces were painted Deck Blue.

The BAGLEY (DD-386), class leader, was camouflaged in Measure 32/1d, the Medium Pattern System. The colors used were Ocean Gray (5-O), Light Gray (5-L), and Dull Black (BK). The deck was painted in patterns of Ocean Gray (5-O) and Deck Blue (20-B). All other horizontal surfaces were painted Deck Blue.

The FINNEGAN (DE-307), an EVARTS Class destroyer escort, was camouflaged in the two-color Measure 32/21d in 1944. The colors used were Light Gray and Dull Black, on vertical surfaces, and large patterns of Ocean Gray and Deck Blue on the deck. Horizontal surfaces were painted in Deck Blue.

Measure 32/3d, the most widely applied of the Medium Pattern Systems, is applied to the DAVIS (DD-395), a SOMERS Class destroyer. The three standard colors used were Ocean Gray, Light Gray, and Dull Black on the vertical surfaces, with the deck painted in patterns of Deck Blue and Ocean Gray, and all horizontal surfaces painted Deck Blue.

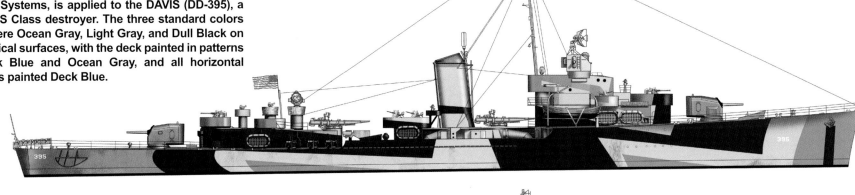

The BLUE (DD-744), an ALLEN M. SUMNER class destroyer, camouflaged in Measure 32/9d, the Medium Pattern System, was named for the BLUE (DD-387) that sank off of Guadalcanal in 1942. The colors used were Ocean Gray, Light Gray, and Dull Black. The deck was painted in patterns of Deck Blue and Ocean Gray, with all other horizontal surfaces painted in Deck Blue.

The COMPTON (DD-705) was camouflaged in Measure 32/11d, the Medium Pattern System, which employed Light Gray, Ocean Gray, and Dull Black. As with the other Medium Pattern Systems, the deck carried a pattern of Ocean Gray and Deck Blue.

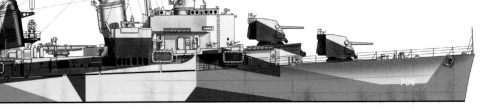

Measure 31, Dark Pattern System

Geometric patterns were first developed and used as camouflage during WWI. Following the end of hostilities in Europe all ships were repainted in the light gray scheme. In the midst of WWII, the Bureau of Construction and Repair again authorized the use of pattern camouflage when it issued *Ships-2 Supplemental* on 1 March 1943.

The first of these pattern systems was designated Measure 31, the Dark Pattern System. The directive called for all vertical surfaces to be painted in a pattern of Haze Gray (5-H), Ocean Gray (5-O), and Black #82. All horizontal surfaces, including the deck, canvas covers, gun mounts, and gun directors were to be painted a pattern of Deck Blue (20-B) and Ocean Gray (5-O). Design sheets were supplied for the port and starboard sides and the deck to be used as a guide in painting. The directive also stated that the camouflage painting need not be exact or carried into the corners. The directive went on to say there would be no objection to careful painting that may be desired for the sake of good appearance at close range.

The designs were specifically drawn for different classes of destroyer, so the measures could,

and often did, differ from class to class. Because of different hull lengths and superstructure designs, the measures for a battleship (BB) would not fit a destroyer (DD) or destroyer escort (DE). Although designs for cruisers (CA/CL) did find their way to destroyers and visa versa.

As to application, considerable artistic license was employed, some due to available paint supplies, and some to the necessity of having the ship ready to sail following refit, when the painting usually occurred. Careful examination of photos of ships painted in the same measure number reveals the extent of interpretation that went into specific applications.

The different measures were designated for different designs within the measure, thus Measure 31/1d was designed for a destroyer and Measure 31/1c was designed for a cruiser, they all however consisted of the same three colors of Haze Gray, Ocean Gray, and Black with a deck pattern of Deck Blue and Ocean Gray.

Most destroyers and destroyer escorts carried one or more of the three 31/33 Measures in late 1943 and 1944, and some into 1945.

The after deck of the MUGFORD (DD-389), tied up at a staging wharf at Mare Island, California, on 5 March 1945, reveals the deck pattern of her Measure 31/1d paint. The light areas are in Ocean Gray (5-O), and the dark areas are in Deck Blue (20-B). Canvas stained Deck Blue covered the 20mm, 40mm, and 5-inch guns. (Floating Dry Dock)

The HOEL (DD-533), a FLETCHER Class destroyer, wears Measure 31/1d, the Dark pattern System. Vertical surfaces were Haze Gray (5-H), Ocean Gray (5-O), and Black. All horizontal surfaces were to be painted in a pattern of Deck Blue (20-B) and Ocean Gray. Japanese warships sank the HOEL off Samar on 25 October 1944. (Floating Dry Dock)

Measure 31/1d is seen here as drawn for the BAGLEY Class destroyer HELM (DD-388), seen here in Mare Island Channel on 28 April 1944 following her refit and repaint. Her pennant number has been painted in white high up on the forecastle. The HELM received 11 Battle Stars for her WWII service in the Pacific. (Floating Dry Dock)

The THATCHER (DD-514) was camouflaged in Measure 31/2c, a scheme that had been designed for a cruiser but adapted to fit the FLETCHER Class destroyer in 1944. This measure employed a geometric design on the port side in the three basic colors of Haze Gray, Ocean Gray, and Black. The THATCHER was hit twice by kamikazes late in the war in the Pacific. (Floating Dry Dock)

The YARNALL (DD-541) was another FLETCHER Class destroyer to be camouflaged in Measure 31/2c. The starboard side design employed a mostly squared-off geometric design, with a few rounded patterns. The YARNALL served in the Pacific all of her career, earning 11 Battle Stars: 9 for WWII, and 2 for Korea. (Floating Dry Dock)

The RICHARD S. BULL (DE-402) is camouflaged in Measure 31/3c, a design that had been adapted from a scheme for a cruiser. The pennant number has been centered on the forecastle hull side in white. A red and white "I have a pilot onboard" flag flies from the halyard. The destroyer escort is armed with a pair of 5-inch guns and numerous 20mm and 40 mm cannons. (Floating Dry Dock)

The HOWARD F. CLARK (DE-533), camouflaged in Measure 31/3c, "rides herd" on an escort carrier in the Pacific in 1944. Her 31/3c paint shows considerable wear, especially at the bow. Many hands are on deck as she approaches another ship to take on mail, personnel, and perhaps a movie. (Floating Dry Dock)

Another example of Measure 31/3c is seen applied to the EVERSOLE (DE-404) in 1944. Considerable latitude was allowed when applying the geometric styles of Measure 31. The Japanese I-45 sank the EVERSOLE, then operating off of Leyte, on 28 October 1944. The EVERSOLE had just undergone a refit at Navy Yard, Boston the previous April 1944. (Floating Dry Dock)

The McCOOK (DD-496), camouflaged in Measure 31/3d steams through rough Atlantic seas in 1944. She participated in the Invasion of Normandy on 6 June 1944 and was rotated back to the United States where she was converted to a destroyer minesweeper (DMS). Measure 31/3d was widely applied to destroyers and destroyer escorts in both the Atlantic and Pacific during 1944. (Floating Dry Dock)

The BUCKLEY (DE-51) was the lead ship in the class and wore Measure 31/3d camouflage in 1944. Measure 31/3d differed from Measure 32/3d in that the port and starboard side designs were different and Haze Gray (5-H) was used on the 31 System and Light Gray (5-L) was used on the 32 System. The BUCKLEY Class was armed with three 3-inch/50 caliber naval guns and was modified by removing the torpedo tubes and substituting additional 20mm and 40mm anti-aircraft guns. (Floating Dry Dock)

The bow of the LARDNER (DD-487) is seen here as she lies off Puget Sound Navy Yard, in Washington on 23 September 1944. She is camouflaged in the Open Measure 31/3d that utilized the three colors of Ocean Gray (5-O), Haze Gray (5-H), and Dull Black (BK) on all vertical surfaces, and Ocean Gray (5-O) in a pattern that carried over the sheer line to the deck, with Deck Blue (20-B) painted on all other deck and horizontal surfaces. (Floating Dry Dock)

The EISNER (DE-192) is camouflaged in a modified Measure 31/3d scheme as it sails out of Navy Yard, New York on 10 July 1944. The angled Black (BK-82) bow stripe has not been added and the Black (BK-82) stripe that terminated at the forecastle is at an odd angle. The EISNER is outfitted with additional radio antennas and a HF/DF antenna on her main pole mast. (Floating Dry Dock)

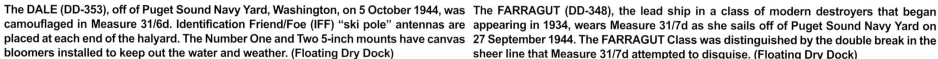

The DALE (DD-353), off of Puget Sound Navy Yard, Washington, on 5 October 1944, was camouflaged in Measure 31/6d. Identification Friend/Foe (IFF) "ski pole" antennas are placed at each end of the halyard. The Number One and Two 5-inch mounts have canvas bloomers installed to keep out the water and weather. (Floating Dry Dock)

The HOPEWELL (DD-681), camouflaged in Measure 31/9d, rides at anchor off an island "somewhere in the Pacific" in 1944. All of her signal flags are flying from her halyards signifying an important event, perhaps Christmas. The port side ship's boat is casting a shadow on the camouflage scheme, changing the design. (Floating Dry Dock)

The FARRAGUT (DD-348), the lead ship in a class of modern destroyers that began appearing in 1934, wears Measure 31/7d as she sails off Puget Sound Navy Yard on 27 September 1944. The FARRAGUT Class was distinguished by the double break in the sheer line that Measure 31/7d attempted to disguise. (Floating Dry Dock)

The BOYD (DD-544) is camouflaged in the Measure 31/10d scheme as drawn for the FLETCHER Class in 1944. Her pennant number has been painted in white, high up on the hull side on the forecastle. Her paint is already beginning to show signs of flaking and damage due to the salt water corrosion conditions of the Pacific. (Floating Dry Dock)

The starboard side of the THOMASON (DE-203), appears camouflaged in Measure 31/16d, as drawn for the BUCKLEY Class in 1943. Her ship's boat has been included in the scheme. The angular patterns drew heavily on the designs that were conceived during WWI. All canvas covers for the exposed 3-inch gun mounts are stained Deck Blue (20-B). (Floating Dry Dock)

Another view shows the BOYD (DD-544) as she sails out of Mare Island Navy Shipyard on 18 March 1944 camouflaged in Measure 31/10d. Bethlehem, in San Pedro, California constructed the BOYD. Her pennant number has been painted at the stern in white. (Floating Dry Dock)

The HOWORTH (DD-592) is anchored off of Puget Sound Navy Yard, Washington on 3 May 1944 camouflaged in Measure 31/21d Mod. The modification to the scheme included the addition of an Ocean Gray (5-0) panel below the black panel on the bow. A black ball in the halyard shows that the HOWORTH is at anchor. (Floating Dry Dock)

The PURDY (DD-734) is seen here as she sails in the Pacific in 1944, camouflaged in Measure 31/25d, a little-used scheme on destroyers. The PURDY was an ALLEN M SUMNER Class destroyer that was constructed by Federal Shipbuilding and Dry Dock, Kearny, New Jersey. Commissioned in 1944, the PURDY was soon sent to war. (Floating Dry dock)

The MASSEY (DD-778), camouflaged in Measure 31/25d, appears in the Pacific in 1944. The Deck Blue (20-B) can be seen on the decks, atop the 5-inch gun mounts, wheelhouse, and all other horizontal surfaces. The aft stack is fitted with a radio direction finder (RDF) antenna. Bethlehem, San Pedro, California built the MASSEY. (Floating Dry Dock)

Measure 32, Medium Pattern System

Measure 32 was also authorized by the 1 March 1943 edition of *Ships-2 Supplement*. It differed from Measure 31 only in the colors utilized. The directive called for painting all vertical surfaces in a scheme of Light Gray (5-L), Ocean Gray (5-O), and Black. The deck and horizontal surfaces, such as gun mounts, torpedo tubes, canvas covers, and gun directors, were to be painted a pattern of Deck Blue (20-B) and Ocean Gray (5-O).

As with Measure 31, design sheets were provided as guides for painting ships in Measure 32. The guides also designated how the paint would be applied into corners and on the sides of gun mounts, stacks, and superstructure areas.

Measure 32 was perhaps the measure most widely used on destroyers and destroyer escorts from 1943 to 1945, with some 30 designs drawn for the ships. In Measure 32, as in Measure 31, the design differed from port to starboard, with the exception of the destroyer JACCARD (DE-355) that carried Measure 32-33/3d in a design pattern that was the same on both sides, but differed in the colors utilized.

All of the Pattern Systems traced their origins to designs initially drawn up during WWI, when some 120 individual patterns were created. The designs were called "dazzle" or "piebald," and were intended to confuse a surface observer as to the course, angle, and speed of a vessel. Most destroyers and destroyer escorts wore one of the three Pattern Systems designed for WWII.

The JOHN M. BERMINGHAM (DE-530) was the last destroyer escort constructed for the U.S. Navy during WWII. She is camouflaged in Measure 32/1d as she sails out of Navy Yard, Boston, on 15 August 1944. The three colors used were Light Gray (5-L), Ocean Gray (5-O), and Dull Black (BK) on vertical surfaces, and Deck Blue (20-B) and Ocean Gray (5-O) on all horizontal surfaces. (Floating Dry Dock)

The BERNADOU (DD-153) was a WICKES Class "flush deck" destroyer that had been converted to an ocean escort by removing one stack and boiler to make room for additional fuel. She is camouflaged in Measure 32/3d. The main mast has been fitted with a Huff/Duff (HF/DF) antenna that was used to detect radio transmissions from German U-Boats. (Floating Dry Dock)

An aerial oblique side view dated 8 October 1944, shows the "flush deck" COLE (DD-155), a WICKES Class destroyer that had been converted to an ocean escort. She is camouflaged in Measure 32/3d, and her Deck Blue (20-B) paint has non-skid panels that lead from the bridge area hatches to the forward (Number One) 3-inch gun mount. The COLE was commissioned in 1919 at Cramp Shipbuilding. (Real War Photos)

The BRISTER (DE-327), outfitted to hunt submarines and escort convoys, is camouflaged in another variation of Measure 32/3d as she sails off Norfolk Navy Yard in July 1944. The painters have interpreted the camouflage scheme, which differs from that on the DAVIS (DD-395) in the application of the black stripe at the bow. (Floating Dry Dock)

The starboard side of the DAVIS (DD-395) is seen after her final refit at Navy Yard, Charleston, South Carolina. The DAVIS was modified with the removal of her Number Two twin 5-inch mount and Number Three twin 5-inch mount, and replaced with a single 5-inch mount. The DAVIS is camouflaged in Measure 32/3d. (Floating Dry Dock)

With the National Ensign flying from the main mast, the destroyer escort EDSALL (DE-152) moves at speed while camouflaged in Measure 32/3d. Measure 32/3d was the most widely used of all of the schemes drawn for destroyers and destroyer escorts from 1943 to 1945. The EDSALL was the lead ship in her class and was armed with 3-inch guns, 20mm and 40mm cannons, Hedgehog launchers, and depth charges. (Floating Dry Dock)

The VANCE (DE-387) operated in Alaskan waters in 1944 while camouflaged in a modified Measure 32/3d scheme, which was designed for the ALLEN M. SUMNER Class in 1943. The U.S. Coast Guard operated the VANCE and many other destroyer escorts during WWII. The VANCE's mid-ships torpedo tubes have been removed in favor of additional anti-aircraft armament. (U.S. Coast Guard)

The LAUB (DD-613) is undergoing the installation of new sea and air search radar antennas at Navy Yard, Boston in November 1944. Her 32/3d camouflage vertical Ocean Gray (5-O) patterns are carried over the sheer line and up to the deck. The top of the forward gun mounts and gun director are painted Deck Blue (20-B). (Floating Dry Dock)

The JOHN HOOD (DD-655), camouflaged in Measure 32/6d, sails in Mobile Bay, Alabama, on 12 June 1944. The sailors are in dress whites in preparation for commissioning ceremonies on 7 June 1944. The JOHN HOOD was constructed by Gulf Shipbuilding in Chickasaw, Alabama and spent all of the war in the Pacific in Alaskan waters. (Floating Dry Dock)

The BRAY (DE-709) is camouflaged in Measure 32/3d, as drawn for a destroyer escort. An additional panel of Light Gray (5-L) was added to the bow area. The BRAY was the last destroyer escort built for the U.S. Navy. The air and sea search radars have yet to be added to the foremast. A Huff/Duff (HF/DF) antenna has been added atop the main pole mast. (Elsilrac)

This is another side view of Measure 32/6d camouflage as it appeared on the CAPPS (DD-550) as she sailed off of the Puget Sound Navy Yard, Washington on 29 March 1944. The CAPPS fought the Axis powers in both the Atlantic and Pacific Oceans. All of her 5-inch enclosed gun mounts have bloomers fitted to keep out the weather. (Floating Dry Dock)

The AUSTIN (DE-15), camouflaged in the intricate scheme of Measure 32/9d, is seen departing the U.S. Naval Dry Docks, Hunters Point, San Francisco, California, in 1944, following an overhaul and refit. She served her entire career operating in the Pacific War Zone. (Floating Dry Dock)

This is a starboard side view of the TWIGGS (DD-591), camouflaged in Measure 32/6d, in 1944. The ship's boat is casting a shadow on the hull side that appears to change the camouflage design. The TWIGGS sank off of Okinawa on 16 June 1945, when a Japanese aircraft first launched a torpedo into her and then crashed into the ship to finish her off. (Floating Dry Dock)

The Open Measure 32/22d is seen as applied to the STRAUS (DE-408), a JOHN C. BUTLER Class destroyer escort. The STRAUS was constructed by Brown Shipbuilding in Houston, Texas, and received three Battle Stars for her service in WWII, mainly in the Pacific Area of Operations. Measure 32/22d utilized the two colors of Ocean Gray (5-O) and Dull Black (BK) on vertical surfaces, with the deck painted in patches of Ocean Gray and Deck Blue (20-B). (Floating Dry Dock)

The JOHN C. BUTLER (DE-339), the lead ship in her class, is seen camouflaged in Measure 32/11d, a scheme drawn for destroyer escorts in 1944. The ship was awarded a Presidential Unit Citation for her actions off of Samar, the Philippines, on 25 October 1944. A Chief Petty Officer has his men assembled on the forecastle for a meeting, perhaps to discuss gunnery training. (Floating Dry Dock)

The JOHN W. WEEKS (DD-701) is being delivered by Federal Shipbuilding and Dry Dock at Kearny, New Jersey to the U.S. Navy on 20 July 1944 - a day before commissioning ceremonies. She is camouflaged in Measure 32/9d as drawn for an ALLEN M. SUMNER Class destroyer. Her air and sea search radar will be installed at a staging wharf. (Floating Dry Dock)

The TAUSSIG (DD-746) takes on a load of torpedoes from Covered Yard Lighter (YF-236) while she rides at anchor off of Navy Yard, New York, on 18 August 1944. Her camouflage Measure is 32/9d. It was customary for ships taking on torpedoes to anchor off the docks for safety reasons. (Floating Dry Dock)

The CASSIN YOUNG (DD-793) is camouflaged in Measure 32/7d, a scheme in which Ocean Gray (5-O) and Dull Black (BK) were used on the vertical surfaces, and Ocean Gray (5-O) and Deck Blue (20-B) were used on all horizontal surfaces. The CASSIN YOUNG has been preserved as a memorial at Boston Navy Yard. (Floating Dry Dock)

The COMPTON (DD-705) was camouflaged in Measure 32/11a as drawn for the ALLEN M. SUMNER Class in 1944. The colors used were Light Gray (5-O), Ocean Gray (5-O), and Dull Black (BK) on vertical surfaces and patches of Ocean Gray (5-O) on the deck, with the rest of the deck and horizontal surfaces in Deck Blue (20-B). The COMPTON was credited with shooting down one Japanese aircraft during the Okinawa Campaign. (Floating Dry Dock)

The TILLS (DE-748) operates in the Pacific in 1944 camouflaged in the open Measure 32/10d as drawn for a destroyer escort. The two vertical colors used were Ocean Gray (5-O) and Dull Black (BK), and the horizontal colors were Ocean Gray (5-O), which can be seen on the forecastle deck at the bow and at the stern aside the port side depth charge roller track, and Deck Blue (20-B). (Floating Dry Dock)

The STACK (DD-406) is camouflaged in Measure 32/11d, as drawn for the BENHAM Class in 1944. The colors used were Haze Gray (5-H), Ocean Gray (5-O), and Dull Black (BK) on vertical surfaces, with the deck painted in patches of Ocean Gray (5-O) and Deck Blue (20-B). All horizontal surfaces, such as the top of the gun mounts, gun directors, and stack trunks, were painted Deck Blue (20-B). (Floating Dry Dock)

A surface view shows the IRWIN (DD-794) camouflaged in Measure 32/13d as drawn for the FLETCHER Class. The colors used were Light Gray (5-L) and Ocean Gray (5-O) on the vertical surfaces and large patterns of Ocean Gray (5-O) that coincided with the vertical patterns, and Deck Blue (20-B) on the remainder of the deck and horizontal surfaces. (Floating Dry dock)

The **MORRISON (DD-560)** was camouflaged in Measure 32/13d when photographed by a U.S. Navy blimp on submarine patrol. The patterns of Ocean Gray (5-O) carry over the bow sheer line to the forecastle deck and other areas where the Ocean Gray touched the sheer line. A Japanese kamikaze sank the MORRISON as she operated off of Okinawa on 4 May 1945. (Floating Dry Dock)

The WICKES (DD-578), a FLETCHER Class destroyer, was named for an earlier WWI flush destroyer that was also the class leader. The WICKES is camouflaged in the open Measure of 32/14d, which used utilized the two vertical colors Ocean Gray (5-O) and Dull Black (BK) on the vertical surfaces and Ocean Gray (5-O) and Deck Blue (20-B) in patterns on the deck. Deck Blue was used on all horizontal surfaces such as gun mounts, gun directors, the top of the wheelhouse, and torpedo tubes. The ship's pennant number has been painted in black. (Floating Dry Dock)

The port side of the NORMAN SCOTT (DD-690) appears in camouflage measure 32/13d, the Medium Pattern System, as she lies at rest off of Mare Island Shipyard, California in October 1944, following a refit for damage received by shore gunfire. Her Captain, Seymour Owens, was killed in the action that took place off of Tinian Island on 24 July 1944. (Floating Dry Dock)

The EVARTS (DE-5) is undergoing a camouflage change from Measure 31/3d, the Dark Pattern system to a Medium Pattern System of 32/14d, as drawn for a destroyer escort in 1944. The EVARTS was the class leader of the new destroyer escort type designed by Gibbs & Cox to a British design. The EVARTS spent her entire WWII career operating in the Atlantic, and earned one Battle Star. (Floating Dry Dock)

The MASON (DE-529), camouflaged in Measure 32/1d, is at sea off of Navy Yard, Boston on 26 May 1944. The MASON became famous as the first U.S. Navy ship to have a predominantly African-American crew. The MASON only wore this Measure until August 1944 when the design was changed to 32/9d. The colors used on 32/14d were Ocean Gray (5-O), Light Gray (5-L), and Dull Black (BK) on vertical surfaces, and Ocean Gray (5-O) and Deck Blue (20-B) on the deck. All other horizontal surfaces were painted Deck Blue (20-B). (Floating Dry Dock)

The BRADFORD (DD-545,) off of San Francisco, California on 7 March 1945, is camouflaged in the two-color 32/21d scheme. The ship's colors of Ocean Gray (5-O) and Dull Black (BK) are being refreshed as indicated by the fresh coat of Ocean Gray and the forward Dull Black swoop that has been outlined prior to painting. The deck was camouflaged in patterns of Ocean Gray and Deck Blue (20-B). (Floating Dry Dock)

The TWINING (DD-540), camouflaged in Measure 32/21d, is seen being guided by a harbor pilot off of Hunters Point, California in 1944. This Measure used the two colors of Ocean Gray (5-O) and Dull Black (BK) on vertical surfaces and Ocean Gray (5-O) and Deck Blue (20-B) in patterns on the deck and Deck Blue (20-B) on all other horizontal surfaces. (Floating Dry Dock)

The BEBAS (DE-10), an EVARTS Class destroyer escort, was camouflaged in the Open Measure of 32/22d as she sailed off of the U.S. Naval Dry Docks, Hunters Point, California in 1944. The colors used were Ocean Gray (5-O) and Dull Black (BK) on the vertical surfaces and Ocean Gray and Deck Blue (20-B) in patterns on the deck. This Measure could be loosely applied and could be adapted as a Measure 31 by substituting Light Gray (5-L) for the Ocean Gray. (Floating Dry Dock)

The **FINNEGAN** (DE-307) was photographed off of Navy Yard, Mare Island, California on 1 September 1944 wearing camouflage Measure 32/21d as applied to an EVARTS class destroyer escort. The Dull Black contrasts with the Gloss Black of the boot topping. The FINNEGAN had just been modified by removing the torpedo tubes and adding additional anti-aircraft armament in their place. (Floating Dry dock)

Measure 33, Light Pattern System

Measure 33 was the last of the three Pattern Systems that were laid out in the 1 March 1943 issue of *Ships-2 Supplemental*. This measure reduced the number of authorized colors to two.

The directive for the measure specified that all exposed vertical surfaces be painted in a pattern of Light Gray (5-L) and Ocean Gray (5-O) and all horizontal surfaces, including the deck, tops of gun mounts and directors, canvas covers, tops of torpedo tubes, and the wheelhouse, be painted in a pattern of Deck Blue (20-B) and Ocean Gray.

It appears that only three destroyers and three destroyer escorts were camouflaged in Measure 33; namely, the GEARING (DD-710) that wore Measure 33a/28d, the ALFRED A. CUNNINGHAM (DD-752) camouflaged in Measure 33a/27d, and the JOHN R. PIERCE (DD-753) painted in Measure 33a/30d. The destroyers carried only the two-color scheme, while the destroyer escorts employed three. As in earlier measures, the patterns differed from port to starboard in all but one design.

The JACCARD (DE-355) was one of the destroyer escorts camouflaged in Measure 32-33/3. It carried different patterns on each side and utilized the 32/3d colors of Light Gray (5-O), Ocean Gray (5-O), and Black to port and Measure 33/3d and the colors of Pale Gray (5-P), Haze Gray (5-H), and Black to starboard. The CROSS (DE-448), another such destroyer escort, carried Measure 33a/31d, and the HODGES (DE-231) was camouflaged in Measure 33/3d with the same design utilized on each side.

The patterns design for Measure 33a resembled the Thayer designs of Measure 16 but had panels of Ocean Gray (5-O) over the basic hull and superstructure color of Light Gray (5-L).

(Left) The JACCARD (DE-355) participated in tests in early October 1944 that compared Royal Navy colors to those used by the U.S. Navy. The JACCARD carried Measure 32/3d to starboard and 33/3d to port. The colors used were Light Gray (5-L), Ocean Gray (5-O), and Dull Black (BK) to starboard and Pale Gray (5-P), Haze Gray (5-H), and Navy Blue (5-N) on the port side. The horizontal surfaces were painted in a combination of Deck Blue (20-B) and Ocean Gray (5-O) The design used was the standard 32/3d, only the colors were changed for the experiment. (Floating Dry Dock)

(Right) The HODGES (DE-231) is unusual is that she carries Measure 33/3d Modified on both the port and starboard side. The colors used appear to be Pale Gray (5-P), Haze Gray (5-H), and Dull Black (BK); the same colors utilized in the October 1944 tests. The HODGES was a RUDDEROW Class destroyer escort whose main armament consisted of a pair of 5-inch guns. (Floating Dry Dock)

The FRANK KNOX (DD-742) operated in the Atlantic Ocean off of Rockland, Maine, in December 1944, camouflaged in Measure 33/28d, a scheme very similar to the Thayer System of Measure 16. The scheme employed the colors of Ocean Gray (5-O), Haze Gray (5-H), and Light Gray (5-O) in a wavy pattern extending from bow to stern. Flying from the halyard is a "B" flag, indicating that the vessel is carrying dangerous goods. (Floating Dry Dock)

The CROSS (DE-448) was camouflaged in Measure 33a/31d in 1945, a scheme that was seldom seen on a U.S. Navy destroyer escort. The angular patterns are unusual and appear to follow Royal Navy designs. The colors used are Ocean Gray (5-O) and Light Gray (5-L,), with the deck painted Deck Blue (20-B). The CROSS earned one Battle Star for her service in the Pacific. (National Archives)

The ALFRED A. CUNNINGHAM (DD-752) was camouflaged in Measure 33/27d as she sailed in New York Harbor on 22 November 1944. The Bethlehem Steel Company house flag flies at the halyard as she makes a delivery cruise from the Staten Island Shipyard. The colors used on 33/27d were Light Gray (5-L), Haze Gray (5-H), and Ocean Gray on vertical surfaces, and Deck Blue (20-B) and Ocean Gray (5-O) on horizontal surfaces. (Floating Dry Dock)

This stern quarter port side surface view of the JOHN R. PIERCE (DD-753) making a delivery cruise off of New York City on 29 December 1944, shows her camouflaged in Measure 33/30d. The scheme employed the standard three colors of Haze Gray (5-H), Ocean Gray (5-O), and Light Gray (5-L). Bethlehem Steel, Shipbuilding Division, Staten Island Yard, New York constructed the JOHN R. PIERCE. (Floating Dry Dock)

The DRAYTON (DD-366) was painted at Pear Harbor, Territory of Hawaii, in an experimental Measure 1B camouflage scheme in 1942. The scheme consisted of an overall Sapphire Blue hull and superstructure, with the decks painted Sea Blue (5-S) and the mast tops in Haze Gray (5-H). (U.S. Navy Via Elsilrac)

The ANDRES (DE-45) was camouflaged in Measure 22, the Graded System, which consisted of Haze Gray (5-H), at the lowest level of the sheer line, and Navy Blue (5-N) below that parallel to the water. The unidentified destroyer escort that is pulling up along side the ANDRES shows the Deck Blue (20-B) atop the forward (Number One) 5-inch mount and the forecastle deck. (U.S. Navy Via Elsilrac)

The BUCHANAN (DD-484) pulls up along side the fleet carrier WASP (CV-7) on 3 August 1942, to take on fuel and supplies, during the Tulagi Island Invasion. The BUCHANAN is camouflaged in a Modified Measure 12 that consisted of Sea Blue (5-S), Haze Gray (5-H), and Ocean Gray (5-O). The lines from the WASP enable the carrier to pull the BUCHANAN along. (U.S. Navy Via Elsilrac).